All In The Mind

Catherine Wain

chipmunkapublishing
the mental health publisher

Published by
Chipmunkapublishing
United Kingdom

http://www.chipmunkapublishing.com

Copyright © 2015 Catherine Wain

ISBN   978-1-78382-221-8

Sammy my last farewell

This is a true story about a dog called Sammy and his
mistress who suffered from a mental illness known as
bipolar disorder when one day Catherine was feeling fed up
living on her own so she decided she wanted a pet dog to
share her life and Sammy was to come into her life a little
six week old puppy it was love at first sight the pair hit it of
straight away Sammy was a cross between a jack Russell
and a Staffordshire bull terrier Catherine knew they were
going to be the best of mates' and she would take Sammy
with her where ever she went on long walks down to the
lakes were they lived and the pair were inseparable a match
made in heaven Catherine couldn't remember the last time
she was so happy Sammy meant the world to her she
treated Sammy like her little baby he was the love of her life'
Sammy was at Catherine's side at all times even when she
was not well Sammy was one in a billion always there when
she needed him he gave her the will to live and everything
was fine for the first few years when Catherine took a turn
for the worse on one fateful night with tragic consequences
on a cold winters night   pouring down with rain when
Catherine walked out her house leaving all the doors open
and Sammy following after her without his lead on Catherine
started to cross the main reservoir road to try and get some
help at the hospital when all of a sudden Sammy ran into the
road and a car knocked him down and killed him the shock
of what happen put Catherine in the hospital that same night
under heavy medication Sammy had given his life to save
Catherine's he was trying to warn her of a car coming and
the car hit Sammy instead of Catherine saving her life and
when Catherine came out the hospital and back to her
empty house without Sammy at her side that night she could
of filled a reservoir full of her tears for the best friend she
ever had who had left a aching wound in her heart and
wished it had been her that had gone under that car and not
Sammy not a day goes by when she is not thinking about
Sammy the love of her life and knows he his in heaven
running around and looking down on her I solute you pal

My last farewell

On that fateful night pouring down with rain
When you slipped away from your chain
Your mistress going out of her brain
Her heart full of sorrow and pain
You was always there by her side
The night you slipped away and died
On The nights that she as cried
That last journey long and wide
So why does she feel mad
Loosing the best friend she ever had
Because Sammy was never bad
Making me feel so very sad
Sammy you have left one big mark
Never hearing you bark
Out alone in the park
Walking alone without you after dark
My lonely journey back home
Where we both used to roam
Oh how my heart aches
Tears filling up our lakes
Ps Sammy the night you died a part of me died
Rest in peace and I salute you
Catherine Wain

Mother Nature

Take one look around and see
What you are doing to me
Killing me slowly bit by bit
Down inside your pit
There is so little time left
Before Mother Nature rears her head
Maybe leaving us all for dead
While sleeping alone in our beds
Earthquakes fires floods and hurricanes
We have seen them all
So before she takes her toll
Lets give Mother Nature one last call
By getting back to our roots
Which is never too late?
Ps oh sorry but nature calls

Autumn

Night times are drawing in
The trees are getting rather thin
Curtains are being drawn
At the crack of dawn
Babies are being born
Mothers tired and worn
Winter is a coming
The trees are now bear
So let's show we care
By sharing a piece of bread
Now that the leaves have all been shed
'Ps don't forget to feed the animals

Birds of prey

Little birds oh so gay
Singing together in the month of May
All playing together on rolls of hay
Ready to stay another day
Blue tits yellow tits
All singing my hits
Never ready to quit
Because they are my biggest hits
Up like a lark
Leaving behind the dark
Listening to the sounds of a dog bark
And all waiting to go on Noah's ark
Good heavens above

My three little birds

Once upon a time lived three little birds
All nesting in there cosy nest
Enjoying a meal from there mom
Ready to fly of to another world
There eyes as big as thunder
And feeling so humble
Ready for that one big stumble
Where my three little birds
Ps if I was to use my loaf would my birds
Mind if there bread was full of doe
Think about it

Dawn chorus

After the sunset
A new dawn begins
Leaving clouds of dust
When they fade into the night
A new dawn is a coming
The morning chorus now in tune
Upon the horizon so very clear
Sounds of trees ever so green
Hustling and bustling
Skies so blue and not a broken cloud
Our feather friends flying so high
Two and throw they begin to sing
And when night time befalls us
The stars appear with that twinkle
Not one sound can be heard
Closing our eyes to such a perfect day
See you tomorrow

Catherine Wain

Bearing fruit

Take one look around and see
Our trees bearing fruit
They say that money does not grow on trees
But food does and lots of it
Enough for everyone
So come on and let's do our sharing
Caring for those who have no fruit
My message for you all

Mother Nature rears her head

Just along the sea shore
Tidal waves big and tall
Black skies full of thunder
Destroying everything in her way
Wind and rain giving us lots of pain
The sun so hot leaving us all to rot
Just another day and another night
Climate change is here to stay
Droughts floods heat waves
This situation is so very grave
So lets give mother nature one last chance
Going back to our roots where it all began
Over to you

Between heaven and hell

Heaven is when a mother gives birth to her first child mother
nature at her best that first seed growing like a flower ready
to bloom in the midday sun such pleasure that tiny bundle of
joy screaming her tiny lungs off for all to hear wrapped inside
her mothers arms a new day begins and a new life begins
and on to her new journey
So lets get back to earth and the other side of nature and the
sheer anger she is unleashing on us all the disasters we are
all witnessing around the world earthquakes floods fires and
tornados a calling we cannot ignore so by getting back to our
roots and looking after that one seed by giving mother
nature one last call
From one seed

The human race

Don't become part of the rat race
Along with all the nut cases
Put on a brand new face
Then go your own pace
We all come into world with nothing
So our journey after birth
Here on this earth
Should be caring for the human race
The hungry homeless sick and old
Which should not be a load to bear?
If we all showed that we cared
A piece of bread in our hands
Ready to feed a empty mouth
There eyes full of tears
Taking away there hunger and pain
This is the human race I want to be part of
A kind caring and sharing one
And enough bread for us all
So use your blooming loaf

Catherine Wain

Down on the funny farm

Where were supposed to feel calm
Feeling free from any harm
Reading the future from our palm
I don't think we are all that bad
May be a little sad
And oh would I feel glad
If I did not feel so mad
So don't just stand and stare
Eyes watching with that glare
To stop me from pulling out my hair
And if we used our brains
To stop going insane
Oh what a thrill
Never taking another pill
Ps I am in two minds whether to give the doctors
A piece of my mind
Think about it

My own medicine

Please will you pull out the plug?
To stop you giving me some of your drugs
Because all we need is one big hug
To stop me feeling like one big mug
You need to get back to school for more education
And one big investigation
Making me take some of your medication
Leaving me hopping mad
Because we are not that bad
So why send in the bill
For not taking your pills
Making me want to give all doctors a piece of my mind
Ps do you get it

Catherine Wain

World at war

In this troubled world of ours
Stand tall inside your boots
Throw away your weapons and guns
Because war will never been won
Let us all show we care
So we don't have to bear
The scars of hatred and war
Which we don't need any more
Praying for a better life for us all
A message is written on the wall
No more tears like falling rain
And no more anger sorrow or pain
So let us all pray for peace
Out in the open breeze
A band of hope a ray of light
Not hearing of another soldier's bloody plight
Make love not war

War prayer

Let's all do our deed
For our family in need
Wiping out this greed
Will someone please lead?
Because war is such a bore
Rotten to the core
Starving our poor
So lets get ready to kick down that door
Ps my message for you all

Imagine

Imagine what the world would be like
If we dropped our weapons of war
And take one look around
To see half the human race
Slowly dying from lack of food and water
That we all take for granted
Let's drop our weapons of war
As war is such a bore
So hope your listening bush and blair
Over to you

Soldier's prayer

Not all men are ready for the kill
After doing there morning drill
Hiding out amongst the hills
Ready for that next kill which is against there will
Now that the deed is done
And no one as won
The roar of a loaded gun
Can be heard in the midday sun
And glory is all thine
Where some of the men have died
There bodies long and wide
Nothing left but there pride

Blue bell woods

Down in blue bell woods
Lies a figure of a man
No one knows where he came from
Nor did anyone ask
Tommy was an old soldier and comrade
A victim from the Second World War
Still building trenches from his enemies
Escaping from life and reality
But Tommy had made lots of friends
Amongst the animals he loved so dear
Waking up to the sounds of birds singing
Up in the trees so ever green
But Tommy's mind was never at peace
The night he slipped away and died
May you rest in peace?
Your war is now finely over
Good night

Troy' ageing van

Is there anyone out there that can?
Ger rid of my son troy's ageing van
You can take it away for free
And it won't cost you a fee
Down to the nearest scrap yard
Where you must be on your guard
Making sure you give it a almighty whack
To stop troy getting back
Troy's van has long past it sell by date
Leaving his van at the pearly gates
Tears of happiness tears of joy
Seeing the back of troy's one big toy
Hoot Hoot

Seed of love

My son troy is still a troubled boy
Trapped inside a man's body
Both mentally and physically
So how do I get through to my son
Who as lost all sense of fun
His mind on the run
Firing bullets with a loaded gun
He hides in his room
Feeling full of doom and gloom
Waiting for his next fix
Making me want to give him one big kiss
Trapped like a prisoner
Destroying his brain cells
Putting me through sheer bloody hell
Making me want to scream and yell
So before we both go insane
Stop and take heed
By not taking this bloody weed

Strings of a guitar

If I fall to sleep
And no one sees me
Please play a tune
On the old guitar
Strings of heaven a boy
Strings of pleasure my troy
Strings of peace such joy
And when I wake up
And you are still playing
The strings of my heart
Grow stronger and stronger
Dedicated to my son troy

Catherine Wain

Daddy's prayer

Daddy Daddy eyes so blue
Let me peep in to give me that clue
Of what you may be going through
Because my love for you will stick like glue
A tear drop is all I need
For you to keep me on that lead
And for giving me the feed I need
Planting your love growing like a seed
To the daddy I never knew
His big old heart oh so true
My tiny feet walking inside his shoes
There were times I needed you
God bless you

Abandon babe

On a cold winters night
The stars are shining bright
May there be some light
On this face oh so white
A Young women so very poor
Waiting by the church door
Her hands freezing cold
Running down the main road
Tears rolling down her face
Where she was all of a daze
After leaving her babe in lace
Praying to god she had not fallen from grace
God bless you both
Ps this poem is close to my heart
Because I was an a abandon babe

Abandon Tim

Who ever abandon tiny Tim?
Where no one could hear his cries
Leaving him so full of fright
Out in the middle of the night
When tiny Tim was found
And not looking to proud
His medical bills may be a few pounds
But who cares now that he his safe and sound
Tiny Tim will need a good home now
A loving family to love and care for him
Running amongst the meadow
Has fast as his tiny legs can run
So who ever betrayed tiny Tim's trust?
Leaving him all alone in that muddy field
Let us show that some one cares
By offering a home for all unwanted pets
Woof Woof the cry of freedom

Woof Woof

Rebel Rebel who walked on air
His heart so full of care
The children loved to pamper him
Just to get his golden hamper
Woof Woof the cry of freedom
For all his pals to hear
Taking away there fears
Who he loved so dear
Rebel rebel his heart made of gold
Keeping his pals away from the cold
And who was always good and never bold
Walking down that narrow road
Ps this poem is dedicated to all animals
With no fixed address tonight
You're all welcome to mine
Woof woof

Some whale of a friend

Up amongst the Yorkshire dales
Lies a doggy wagging his tail
Feeling free out of his jail
Writing about his own little tale
About his master swigging back the ale
Looking rather thin and pale
After standing on a dirty nail
Ready to read his daily mail
His faithful doggy by his side
After his master slipped and died
No where left to hide?
Only the tears that he cried
So he was some whale of a friend
Woof woof

My best pal

Boris has left his mark
Making me want to nark
No more walkies out in the park
Making him want to bark
Because he never moans
playing with lots of stones
While talking down the phone
With my friend so dear
Sipping my pint of beer
Feeling calm and out of fear
Woof Woof music to my ear

Catherine Wain

Sunny

To my furry old friend Sunny
With his big sticky up ears
And yes' at times he can be naughty
and will always be my number one
Sunny loves to go on his daily walks
Down to the nearest park
Running after his tiny ball
Jumping over the nearest wall
And when night times fall
And sunny is ready to crawl
On to his mistress bed
Ready to stay another day
Ps sweet dreams Sunny

Doggy tale

little Boris gives me such pleasure
While walking him in my leisure
He loves to chat to his mates
Barking over the garden gate
The children love to play with him
While working out at the local gym
They begin to throw his ball
Boris jumping over the nearest wall
He loves to play all day at his local park
Listening to lots of doggy barks
Two and throw he wags his tail
While his mistress reads his favourite tales
Ps to any doggy without a home tonight
You're all welcome to come to mine

Catherine Wain

Running bare foot

When I begin my journey
Through meadows pastures and green
Crossing over many rivers
Water running down the streams
The rustling of the trees
So very green in the midday sun
And all the animals grazing on the land
Making me feel great to be alive
Oh so pure oh so simple
Has nature had intended
Running naked through the fields
Oh such freedom away from it all
And when night times fall
And the birds have stopped calling
Across the arisen where all is calm
Until the morning light where there all singing in tune
Tweet tweet

Cries of a nation

Africa Africa a land so true
With a feeling oh so blue
Stand tall inside your shoes
My message for you all
Just how I see
What is troubling me?
Tired eyes looking at trees
Stinging like a Bee
Babies weak with hunger
Clinging to breast like thunder
Trying hard to fill there tiny beaks
There plight oh so bleak
We must all try in vain
Hands wrapped around in chains
There hearts and souls full of pain
On land dry with out rain
Ps can you help?

Our family in need

For every penny spent on a church building
Another hungry child as died some where in Africa
So what would my own religion be?
Just to feed an empty mouth
A penny well spent
I hope some one is listening out there
To just show you care
And another child does not have to die
Of hunger pain and starvation
Over to you

Staff of life

What must it be like?
Never tasting a slice of bread and butter
Out in the poor parts of Africa
A bacon or chip butty
We have never had it so good
A piece of grain is like gold dust
We don't know how our bread is buttered over here
So don't let another hungry child die
Let us do our sharing
By caring for those who have nothing
My message just for you

Catherine Wain

Cries for help

Why oh why
Is my land so dry?
My eyes full of tears making me want to cry
My body laid down ready to die
Feeling tired and beat
No harvest crops or wheat
Nothing left for us to eat
So before laying down to rest
Deep down in my little nest
Could you spare a few pounds?
Getting our feet back of the ground
By planting our crops again
Praying for some rain
To ease some of our pain
Thank you

There last journey

Let us all cherish
Those who did not perish
Out On the deadly seas
Stinging them like a bee
Fleeing from terror and wars
Dozens by the score
There bodies now tired and worn
Just let's open our doors
Letting them live in peace
Where they no longer need to weep
Now feeling so calm
Away from any harm
No longer living in fear
After shedding so many tears
So let's show we care
A cross we all have to bear
Ps To all those that did not make that last journey
You are all now in the lords house   RIP

City lights

Down in the city
Where the lights are not so pretty
Too many people what a pity
All rushing around with no were to go
And if we stopped for one minute
And take one look around and see
A little old lady
Her clothes tatted and worn
Sleeping rough on the city streets
If we could open our eyes
By helping out the homeless
All sleeping rough on our city streets tonight
Ps please show that you care
If we offered our hand in friendship

Face in the window

On a cold winters day
Sits a man all alone
Very far from home
Drinking his half mug of tea
Lots of people pass him by
Never giving him a second glance
This lonely figure of a man
Sat staring through a window pane
If for one second we found the time
By sharing that half mug of cold tea
With bill the face in the window
There would be no more sad faces
Ps and it would be hot teas all around
Cheers

Catherine Wain

Fools Alley

Swilling back the beers inside there bellies
While sat in front of the telly
Go get another beer Kelly
My head feels like a lump of jelly
After drinking a few jars
And driving in there car
Looking for the nearest bar
So drunk he was seeing stars
So just for kicks
Smashing windows with a brick
And getting lots of stick
Down at the nearest nick
Cheers

Eyes that see

Kitty kitty her bite soft as grit
Her eyes full of fire ready to be lit
For all to see inside her kit
Because she is one of my biggest hit
Kitty kitty oh so slick
and I know just how you tick
Making me run to the nearest nick
To stop you from giving me some of your stick
Kitty kitty if only you could see
Showing your love inside of me
Thanks for planting that seed growing like a tree
Hoping it will set you free
Ps dedicated to one hell of rebel
Kitty 85 years young may god be with you

Sleep well Josie

Oh my sweet little child
If only I could find
What is on my mind?
My love for you will never go blind
Little Josie holding a bunch of roses
Lying snug and cosy
For someone as pretty as Josie
Her hair long and shining
Like the stars in her eyes
One look and your on another planet
Heaven where she belongs
Dedicated to Josie
Who was born into poverty?
And died in poverty
Did anyone care?

Through the shadows of darkness

Into the shadows of darkness
May I see some light?
My fight reaching its height
Being given the last rights
In the middle of the night
My soul laid down to rest
My journey about to begin
Through the shadows of brightness
On to ever lasting peace
Good night and god bless

Mp's and there perks

We all know why MP'S are on the fiddle
Court with there trousers down
making them want to piddle
some of us have to work for a crust
To stop us from going so very bust
For years you have never had it to good
So nip your expenses in the bud
By going out to work like the rest of us
Getting out of your cars and jumpping on the number 11 bus
You were elected to represent the people
Not your family and friends
But now you're running out of luck
By not making a fast buck
We the tax payers want a rebate
For living of the back of the state
So stop taking us for a load of prats
By nicking all of our bread
You Bunch of dirty rats
Order now

The moral law

Why have the banks been so greedy?
Robbing us the very poor
So why should we bail them out
Making us the tax payers scream and shout
Now that we own some of these banks
Making the fat cats walk the plank
Of they go out on there tails
Straight to the nearest jail
The sky high interest they used to charge
There credit way to large
They did get to big for there boots
Pinching all of our loot
So is our money safe any more
Or should we hide it under the kitchen floor
Oh I hates these bankers
Who are a load of W?
Ps Hang your head in shame

Credit crunch

We all know the credit crunch
Is biting all very hard
People abandoning there animals by the score
Making me feel so very sore
These animals are wondering our streets
With little or nothing to eat
Just pining for there masters
Another victim of the credit crunch
Our animals can be our best friends
In times of trouble and need
We love to watch them play in the dirt
And the credit crunch need not have to hurt
So come on and show you care
Keeping our animals free from harm
Money maybe a little tight
But the credit crunch need not have to bite
Woof woof the cry of freedom

Payday loans

Makes me want to moan
By taking there bait
Charging us all with there high interest rates
They pick on the weak
Who already are up the creek?
So who is to blame?
Putting these greedy men to shame
So give us a break
By not making us want to shake
For taking such a big slice of the cake
Hoping all your profits keep you awake
Let's hope there's no rest for your breed
For doing such a bad deed
Being so full of greed
For robbing those in need
Ps got your number

Pressure

Getting out of bed each day
Just to earn a decent pay
Still can't afford to pay my bills
Getting ready for the next big chill
Cuts cuts and more cuts a load to bear
So let the bankers take there share
These cuts are gonna hurt
Ripping the threads of my shirt
I worry what tomorrow will bring
Having one last fling
But it's going to be one big sting
Flying high upon a pair of wings
Only to be bought down with a bump
Back to earth with a jump
And who would I like to thump
Yes these greedy bankers
Ps and now where all paying
You greedy b?

A change gonna come

What a breath of fresh air
To see a friendly black face
Entering the white house
Getting ready for the big race
Upon his broad shoulders
Barrack obama will have to get a lot bolder
By getting the troops out of irac
Being the leader of the pack
A new world and a new nation will be born
At the crack of dawn
We will no longer mourn
The passing away of our dear troops
A few tears have been shed
Alone at night while sleeping in there beds
Praying for peace and harmony
For all the victims of these bloody wars

Freedom

Freedom is to unlock your doors
And to throw away the keys
Talking to our neighbours again
Making a new start and making new friends
Freedom is helping one another
Being able to walk down the street
Never having to look over your shoulders
Freedom is talking to our parents again
Instead of on a mobile phone
Respecting our parents and saying sorry
And saying how much you love them
Freedom is running on a beach
Blue skies above soft sand below
Dogs barking in the midday sun
Running free out of there collars and leads
Freedom is for everyone to be free
From wars crime greed and hatred
We are all humans here on earth
So let's look after Mother Nature
By planting that one seed

Why

Why is life so cheap?
Why do our kids kill other kids?
Not with toy guns
But real guns
Walking the streets at night
May not be so very bright
Being court up in one all mighty fight
Maybe given the last rites
Praying for the dead and wounded
Another child another son
A life so young and gone forever
Oh what a shame
So where did it all go wrong?

Who's to blame?

Knife crime is a sign of our times
Who is to blame for this?
Parent's teachers were all to blame
So let's go back to the drawing board
To learn to respect one another
And the value of life
Instead of using that knife
To take away another young life
By offering your hand in friendship
And throwing away your weapons
So another young child does not need to die
Making us all want to cry
Such a great shame a young child dying alone
Calling for out his mother 'not all kids are the same
You kids have a lot of growing up to do
And think before you get your weapons out
Because the next victim could be you
From one mom

Under lock and key

When night times begins to fall
And foot steps can be heard along the hall
Big men can be heard to cry tears
Locked away in there cells full of fear
There freedom may have gone
Knowing what they did was wrong
Now working in the nick for a couple of bob
A lot better then being on the rob
When morning comes and the screws unlock the cell doors
The inmates begin to sweep there cell floors
Praying for the day when they will get out
Dreaming of driving around the nearest roundabout
They may be under lock and key
Stinging like a bee
But think of the poor victims of there crimes
Who also are doing there time?
Freedom for us all

All lace and nets

Oh how I can bet
Who is looking through her lace nets?
That nosey old Mrs Brown
Wearing that same old frown
Mrs Brown can be so mean
Living of sausage and beans
Thinking it funny
Counting out all her money
Her lace nets might have seen better days
Watching her neighbours at play
And why does she look so mad
If her face didn't look so sad
There must be a Mrs Brown in every street
That think we are all cheats
And yet I cannot help feeling sorry for her
Looking through her lace nets all through the year
God bless her

My benches

While sitting alone in the dark
On my benches out in the park
Listening to the sound of a dog bark
Leaving nothing but there mark
Shock horror
Only to find my benches nicked
By thieves out for there kicks
If only I could see how they tick
They would get some of my stick
Those benches where for my bot
Feeling oh so tired and hot
I would love to give you some of my pot
And hope you forever rot you rotter
Beware thieves
PS these benches where stolen
From the local day centre

Mean cop

My old man's a mean cop
When up in his arms he begins to flop
Two and throw he begins to drop
Leaving me to run and hop
He has an arresting soul
That leaves me burning like coal
When cold feet he hides in a hole
For me to draw the blooming dole
When up in the arms of the law
I am a prisoner oh so raw
I would love to punch him in the jaw
To release the strings of my bow
PS I bet that hurt

My mean landlord

There was a landlord from Kent
Who was so mean he lived in a tent?
At no time was he ever a gent
Making me pay his sky high rents
He was never shy
Making me want to cry
Eating some of his humble pie
Ready to wave bye bye
While counting out his cash
Eating his sausage and mash
Making a dash for the door
Feeling pleased for robbing the poor
He never paid his taxes
With the tax man on his trail
Let's hope he ends in jail
You dirty rotter

Boozy tale

I never did like the taste of booze
Having such a sweet tooth
I found the taste to bitter
Tetley teabags more my tipple
Beer makes me feel so queer
After a few sips and falling of my stool
And feeling such a bloody fool
While falling into the swimming pool
Making me feel oh so cool
Ps good job I am tea total
cheers

Bitter ted

There was a old man called ted
Who was always out of his head?
Never going to bed
Dossing down inside his shed
Ted was a lonely old soul
Booze taking the final toll
After having his last fall
Crawled just like a ball
Drinking was his only escape
After loosing all of his mates
So why was he so full of hate
Smashing all his dinner plates
There is only one road to hell
Ringing out those bells
Drowning inside his wishing well
Ted's body lying stiff
God rest his soul
When you fall there is only one way up
Back on your feet where you belong

Last orders

Please forgive me from falling from grace
Because this could be my last race
I know I am on the brink
Making this my very last drink
Booze is the name of the game
Putting me though such shame
Walking home late at nights
Not feeling to bright
I would love to be in control of my life
Staying at home with my beloved wife
And not down at the nearest bar
Drinking myself silly and seeing lots of stars
So for my family's sake
I need to begin to wake
So no more booze which should be my fate
Which is never too late?
3 cheers

Blind date

While waiting for my fate
Going on my first date
Wishing he would take the bait
Because we could never be mates
he gives me one single rose
While blowing his runny nose
Then he drops of into a dose
His face set in that pose
Feeling like a mug
His feet fixed under my rug
And looking neat and snug
Getting ready to pull out that plug
Bye Bye boring Paul
Like a baby ready to crawl
Ready to knock down that wall
Making me feel ten feet tall
Ps I should have gone to spec savers

Catherine Wain

Battery hens

Why are hens slowly dying?
Cooped up in there darken pens
One light shining throughout the night
the hens not feeling so very bright
Please give our hens back there dignity and freedom
To stop there suffering and pain
To all you farmers out there
Here's my message just for you
Unlock the hen's cages and set the birds free
Roaming around the nearest tree
Leaving behind there darken days
A price worth paying
Ps free range eggs for us all now
Chuckle chuckle

Ding dong

Flirty den
Writing with his pen
At the stroke of ten
To the chimes of big Ben
Tick tock tick tock
This old clock is ready to rock
Down by the docks
Boats ready to sail
Hanging out there tails
Sailors happy' drinking all the ale
Getting a ticket out the local jail
On a crest of a wave
Having a right old rave
And oh what a close shave
For being so brave

Time is running out

Time is running out
Tick tock tick tock
All the clocks ticking together
Soon all these clocks will stop
When mother earth will be no more
Just a pile of ash and rubble
All four seasons rolled into one
At the hands of Mother Nature
So let's turn back the clock
Before Mother Nature puts us in the dock
By getting back to our roots
Mother Nature where it all began
Anyone listning

The anger of the sea

The day the sea died
Along with the cries of the people
Of all ages rich ones poor ones
Old and young
All now resting in god's house
so not all was lost
The day the sea died
Rest in peace

Catherine Wain

The last voyage

Deep down on the ocean floor
Lies a ship and all those that perish
Rich one poor ones old and young
All sailing to a new life
But on that fateful night
Long and wide on the troubled seas
Everyone happy and smiling
On there last voyage
When the ship hit a large ice berg
Slowly the ship went down
To the bottom of the sea
The sea can tell many a tale
On that cold freezing night
Tales of bravery tales of friendship
No one was rich or poor that fateful night
And may god rest there weary souls
God bless you all

Floods of my tears

Tears of anger tears of sadness
My tears pouring down like rain
Nothing left but sorrow and pain
So lay my body down to rest
There will be many rivers to cross
With lots of families bearing there loss
No where left to hide?
With nothing but there pride
When night times fall
And no one hears my call
Please god I am talking to you
Giving me a clue at just what to do
Trying hard to keep my hunger at bay
Digging deep down in the mud and clay
Please shine a light on me tonight
Because the days are now so dark
Dedicated to the victims of the
Pakistan disaster floods may god be with you all

Blowing of steam

The high price of oil
Is making my blood boil
When is this nightmare coming to an end?
Driving us all around the bend
How on earth do we pay our bills?
When were being held against our will
Doesn't any one care about the poor?
Who are feeling so very raw?
How long can this go on?
Feeling cheated and conned
Children going hungry all through the night
Right until the morning light
The poor are getting poorer
And the rich are getting richer
Everything has gone through the flaming roof
Nothing left for a rainy day
Ps it never rain's but it pours
Ps Give us a break

Cold hands warm hearts

Has the days are getting colder
And we are looking older
Just looking over our shoulder
And feeling slightly bolder
And as we creep inside our beds
After we have all been fed
My woolly hat upon my head
My eyes feeling like lumps of led
And when I fall to sleep
Counting all those flaming sheep
Not one little peep
Only the sound of a heart beep
My first cuppa of the day
Looking at the weather oh so gray
Fighting of those winter blues
Reading my mail Sat down on the down stairs loo
Roll on summer

Black skies

Has my body lays down to die
Under the midnights sky
My eyes beginning to cry
When I lie down to die
Just getting away from this hell
My thoughts rushing down that well
And when I begin to fall
Saying good bye to you all
My mind now at ease
To which I am very pleased
No more going round the bend
My journey now at end
Good night

Spaghetti junction

Spaghetti junction leaves one bitter taste
Cars going out of control polluting the air
Who ever built this monster?
Did not have our wild life at heart
Or the folks who live there
One ugly sight to see
Shame on you city planers
Putting cars before people
And if I had my way
I would ban all cars on mars
Spaghetti junction has so many cracks
Making me want to give it an almighty whack
So down with this monster
And all the politicians
Ps you're all grounded

Catherine Wain

Jumble sales

Please bring back the good old jumble sales
Where you never ever fail
To save yourself a couple of bob or two
Waiting for your turn in the nearest queue
What ever the weather
Sunshine or rain
Where in it together standing tall
Oh do I love a bargain
Where most items are a few pence
Making me want to jump over the nearest fence
To be at my local jumble sale
Ps bring back the jumble sales
Or else

Queen of hearts

Why do I find it hard
To play this deck of cards
My heart broken in two
Making me feel oh so blue

Still waiting for a diamond for my finger
My mind all of a linger
With Jack being so very sly
Making me just want to cry

Jack says he would treat me like a queen
Living in his castle like a princess
And promise to sing lots of love song
Playing on his harp and fiddle

So why do I need a club
Just To knock out his lights
Jack being such a cheating love rat
So got myself a spade to bury him

And now I am the queen of the castle
Where you never mess with the ace card
And now the joker is on you
So Now who is the king of the castle
ME
Catherine Wain

Big brother

Why are we being spied on?
By big brothers beady eyes
And do we need all these cameras
Invading our every day lives
Weather it's for dropping down litter
Or smoking in a bus shelter
The county as gone mad
And I thinks it's so sad
My freedom as been taken away
By big brother watching me each day
So to hell with the lot of you
For making me feel oh so blue
Every ctv cameras should call a truce
Putting it to better use
No big brother calling the shots
Because the public are now boiling hot
Ps bring back the old brownie

Television

In the corner of my room
Stands a great big box
Full of doom and gloom
About the news across the world
I feel the soaps have lost there bubbles
Coronation Street gets me of my seat
While running fast on my feet
And Emerdale should be on bail
For leading me of the rails
These soaps have become stale
While listening to there silly tales
So let's send in the bill
Who are out for the kill?
We should get back a rebate
Which is never too late?
Let's hope all the bubbles have now finely burst
From one Television licence payer
Over to you

Don't start

George has given up the weed
After smoking forty fags a day
Looking rather thin and pale
After being let out his jail
No longer a prisoner
Chains have now all gone
Feeling free now that he has won
His battle against the weed
Ps didn't last long

Up in smoke

George used to smoke forty fags a day
And could see me loosing my rag
His eyes looking like bags
So confiscated his jag
To stop him looking like a hag
Making him listen to some of my gags
So he began to nag
With one big snag
With the pair of us having a fag
Ps if you can't beat them join them

No smoke without fire

Feeling oh so glum
Chewing on that nicotine gum
Drowning my sorrows with two tots of rum
While falling down on my bum
I need a smoke before this flaming ban
To which I am not a fan
Good heavens no more cigs
Making me want to do the Irish jig
So gone of in a huff
After having my last puff
And Feeling a bit chuffed
For being so tough
Well if you can't beat em
Join em HELP
there's no smoke with out fire

Roar of a tiger

Bob seger the man's so eager
If I gave him my hand
Would he bring me in the band?
For all to hear throughout the land
Silver and gold the man's so bold
And as me gripped in his hold
Because he's worth his weight in gold
Bob seger his voice full of charm
When listening makes me feel so calm
And has me eating out of his palm
Making me feel safe from any harm
Bob seger gives me much pleasure
While listening in my leisure
Feeling as light as a feather
Wrapped around a bunch of heather
Dedicated to the one and only master Bob seger
Who loves you babe

Music to my ear

Listening to good music
Is like music to my ear
Then I go of to sleep
On a very high note
The sounds of today
Should be kept at bay
Making me feel oh so gray
Because the edges are a little fray
Yesterday's music was the best
Riding high upon that crest
So lay today's music down to rest
Come and snuggle inside my nest
Long live rock en roll

Baby talk

Children Children that I see
Give me your hand
And I will set you free
On to my land worth a couple of grand
Babies feeling happy
Wrapped around there nappies
Before going stark raving potty
Bearing there tiny botty's
Kids of wonder
Big as thunder
You're never a miss
So give me one big kiss
From one big kid

Post man Phil

Post man Phil
When climbing that hill
Gives me one big chill
When delivering my bills
With a licence to kill
He would get one of my pills
Making him pay for all my bills
Giving me the greatest thrill
Naughty naughty

Old Mother Hubbard

Old Mother Hubbard
Went to her cupboard
To find they where bare
Her eyes fixed in that glare
While pulling out her hair
So just for a dare
She stole her fare
To go back home to a place so rare
Where she knew that someone would care
Well done Mother Hubbard
And she lived happy ever after

Burning flame

Burning flame oh so hot
My hate for you never forgot
My babe lying in that cot
For you to burn the bloody lot
Burning flame full of fire
where your still one big liar
You made my life a living hell
Making me want to scream and yell
Burning flame about to thaw
With a feeling oh so raw
You will hurt me like before
Because you are rotten to the core
My candle burning bright
All through these lonely nights
Nothing left but to fight
My rights you took away that flaming night
Ps the truth is out there

All our yesterdays

Life was a lot slower when listening to the sound of big Ben
our entertainment was singing around an old piano down at
the local pub and oh did we have fun singing after dark
maybe a little merry after a few sherries and our parents
waiting up for us and wanting to know all about our evening
out so pure so simple Tommy would spend the rest of the
night sitting on the out side loo reading bits of news paper
we all used as toilet paper I think most of us where educated
in our out side loo's reading the daily mail we may not have
a lot in those days but by god we were happy our mom's
making a stew out of left over's these mums were the
champions of there days trying hard to make ends meet not
having many pounds but oh was they proud so keep smiling
and I salute you all well done

Piggy's last supper

Baby pig= what's for supper tonight ma
Mama pig= egg and bacon
Papa pig=oh I am so hungry that I could eat a horse
Mama pig= don't be so greedy pa and hand around the pork
scratching
Papa pig = if baby pig has to many he will not eat his supper
tonight
Mama pig=it's your excuse to eat the lot
Baby pig= hurry up ma with my supper
Mama pig= coming son and get around the table
Papa pig= will you put extra rashes of bacon on my plate
Baby pig= and on my plate to ma
Mama pig= yes and I have a nice treat for you both some
extra crackling of the pork joint I cooked early on and saved
it for your supper tonight
Baby pig= oh I do love you ma
Papa pig= you are one in a million ma thanks for saving our
bacon
Baby pig= thanks a lot ma is there any more crackling
Papa pig= that was a smashing meal ma
Mama pig =pleased you both enjoyed the meal tonight
tomorrow's supper will be pork chops and belly draft
Baby pig had the biggest smile on his face and fell fast
asleep dreaming of his next meal

The end

The sea monster

Beneath the ocean waves way down on the sea bed lived a
family of fishes all swimming happy together and not a care
in the world Mama fish would always tell her family not to
stray to far away where there was a big sea monster lurking
beneath the deep waters waiting for his next meal and to
swim has far away as possible if you see him one day baby
fish did stray from his home and could not see the dangers
lying beneath the sea bed and went straight in to the path of
the sea monster Mama fish could hear her baby son crying
helplessly and went to rescue him from the jaws of the sea
monster when all of a sudden the sea monster started to
open his big jaw and let one big sneeze out and blew both
mama fish and baby fish all the way back home where the
rest of the family where waiting to greet them and baby fish
never strayed from his home again and they all
Lived happy ever after

The End

The mystery tree house

Once upon a time lived a little boy called josh who was so full of mischief and wonder josh lived in the woods with his grandpa and pet dog sunny where they both loved to roam One day while out playing in the woods josh stumbled across an old tree house were he was full of joy and excitement josh began to explore this tree house with sunny by his side he came across a old trunk with lots of exciting goodies inside it when all of a sudden sunny began to bark and a tall man standing in the door way shouting in a loud voice asking josh what he was doing in his tree house josh got a bit frighten and said how sorry he was and could he go back home to his grandpa the man looked josh straight in the eye and asked if he was on his own yes said josh then I will tell you some stories about my life on the seas both of them began to sit down and the man told josh his name was charley then he began to tell josh about his tales on the seas josh was enjoying charley's stories so much that he forgot the time and begged charley to let him come back soon for more stories they had become the best of friends and when josh got back home he was so full of excitement telling his grandpa all about his new friend Charley. That night' josh could hardly sleep all he wanted to do was to see his friend again in the tree house. Next morning bright and early josh and sunny are of on there travels when they got to the tree house the tree house was no longer there it had vanish with tears of sadness and tears in his eyes josh found a note stuck to a tree which read
Thanks for making a lonely old fool happy and listening to my stories I salute you josh
Charley had gone to the big tree house in the sky and telling his stories to lots of boys and girls across the land

The end

The bag lady

Meg could be seen often walking along the street with all her worldly goods tucked into her carrier bags inside a shopping trolley she could be seen pushing the shopping trolley along the high street singing her head of and the police often moving her on she would always come back, to rest her weary feet on park benches during the day and sleep rough on the same benches at night time passersby would often give her food to eat but Meg would much prefer to rummage through the bins of her local supermarket for food. No one knew where she came from. They were used to seeing her around and Meg was the talk of the neighbourhood she always had a smile on her face and could be seen singing out aloud when she had one to many. One day a young boy playing in the park noticed Meg fast asleep on the benches and went over to talk to her he asked what her name was. Meg is my name and what is your name. Danny' and I live just across the road and come into the park every day to play with my friends Danny asked Meg if he could build her a den to keep her warm. And out the wind and cold a few days later Danny had made the best den in the park a den fit for a queen they had become good friends and Danny would fetch Meg food from his house to give to her One day Danny went to see his friend Meg but she was not there so he went to look for her and found her slumped on the floor with all her worldly goods scattered around her another women was going through her things he shouted at this women to leave Megs possessions alone when she ran of. Danny noticed amongst Megs possessions was a locket and gold chain when Meg got to her feet Danny asked who the man was inside her locket Meg turn round and said if I don't trust you now I never will. The man in the locket was my childhood sweet heart he went of to war and never came back he was killed in action. We was to be married when he came home but he never made it and I have never forgotten him he was the love of my life 'Danny asked what his name was, Harry' she replied and I was heart broken I have been a drifter ever since moving from town to town trying to escape the past. Danny had big old tears in his eyes and asked Meg to move into his house if he asked his mum's permission that's kind of you Danny but I am used to the road it makes me feel free and independent thanks for all your kindness then she gave Danny an envelope not to be open until he got back home and of they parted company both going there separate ways that night Danny open the envelope to find two gold sovereign and a note which read thank you for the best home I ever had you built the best den for miles around which kept me warm and dry so don't ever loose your sense of adventure or your big heart thanks a million from one very happy old lady

The end

Ward 11

Is a ward for
people with mental health problem?

Beth=has anyone got a spare fag
Nurse pots = stop asking for cigarettes from the other
patience's and don't be looking in the ash trays for nub ends
Beth=leave me alone potty
Ed case=is anyone up for a fight what about you Peter
Peter= sorry Ed I have just polish my nails
Smithy= well I hope they crack like your brain
Peter= some ones in a bad mood go and give Beth a
cigarette to stop her going mad
Smithy= it will cost her 'if I lend you a fag Beth I want five
back
Beth= that's day light robbery your just has bad as a
politician robbing the poor to give to the rich
Smithy= maybe I was a bit mean here you are have a couple
of fags on me
Beth=thanks Smithy you have saved my life
Peter= look what you have done now Beth you have ruin his
hard reputation
Ed case= is anyone up for a fight now
Smithy= give it a rest Ed you are getting on my nerves
Nurse pots=come along now boys and girls it is time for your
medication get ready to queue up in a proper line and Peter
you stay in the boys queue
Peter = that's not fair the girls always come first Beth will
you swap places with me if I give you a fag
Beth= you don't smoke
Peter= 'no but I know a man that does
Ed case= what we need is a good fight
Peter= go to bed Ed
Nurse pots= all of you go to bed now and lights out in 10
minutes and no smoking after lights out
Peter= will you tuck me in nurse I have come over funny all
of a sudden
Ed case= what about me nurse I need a good nights story
read to me

Nurse pots= you will get more then a good night story if you don't all get into bed Smithy I hope you have not been smoking because you know the rules about smoking after your medication at 10 o clock

Smithy= sorry nurse but I needed a smoke being locked up with all these loonies

Peter= speak for your self Smithy

Next morning

Nurse pots= doctor Ali would like to see you all after breakfast so stay in the ward and don't sneak of to the shops Smithy you will be in first

Smithy= thanks nurse

The doctor has now arrived and smithy is the first to go in

Doctor Ali= how are you today Smithy are you still hearing voices

Smithy = yes doc

Doctor Ali= and what are the voices saying

Smithy= to punch Peter brown's lights out

Doctor Ali = and why do the voices want to punch Peter's lights out

Smithy= because he gets on my nerves

Doctor Ali=keep on taking your medication and learn to get on with Peter no one is perfect send Beth in now

Beth= I am feeling depressed doctor

Doctor Ali= what is the reason for your depression

Beth= because I have no fags

Doctor Ali= you know that smoking is bad for you and if you don't stop you will go up in a puff of smoke and there will be no more Beth

Beth= I would rather die happy then miserable

Doctor Ali= try chewing gum

Beth= chewing gum makes me feel so glum

Doctor Ali= you are not trying hard enough I will increase your medication send Peter in now

Doctor Ali= hello Peter and how are you today

Peter= one of my nails broke today and some one as stolen my hair straightness I think it is that Beth Watson who as stolen them along with my nail vanish

Doctor Ali= you need to report your loss to the nurse any thing else troubling you Peter

Peter = my nerves are bad and I feel worse then ever

Doctor Ali= you need to relax more go and join the
relaxation class send in Ed case now
Ed case= I am in the mood for a good fight doc it warms me
up and I feel on top of the world
Doctor Ali= you need to calm down Ed and read more books
it is very good for the brain
Ed case=I can't concentrate I get to excited
Doctor Ali= well go of and fight your own demons and I will
see you in a few days time
Next day
Nurse pots= I want you all to join the relaxation classes
today
Beth= the only thing that relaxes me is a good smoke
Smithy will you borrow me a fag until I get my giro
Smithy= yes but don't think I am an easy touch
Beth = thanks a lot
Nurse pots= stop cadging Beth and get ready for the class
Beth= yes nurse
In the keep fit class
Nurse pots= come along every one and begin to jog on the
spot get those legs moving up and down now bend over and
touch your toes let me see you sweating that was great now
lie down on your mats and relax close your eyes and listen
to the sounds of the waves rippling in the water birds singing
in the sky go into a deep sleep and think of the good things
that have happen to you
Peter= oh my god what is that smell
Smithy= don't look at me
Ed case= where ever you may be in church or chapel let it
rattle
Peter=nurse may I be excused from the class the smell is
over powering
Nurse pots= you may Peter
Smithy= and take the smell with you
Peter= cheeky bugger
Nurse pots= the rest of you can carry on so close your eyes
and just drift of to sleep stop the giggling in the corner the
class as finish for one week now so get ready for your next
class see you all next week
Smithy= who ever dropped one in the class done us a
favour it got rid of that moaning peter brown

Ed case= it was him that done one that was why he left the class early I could smell him a mile away

Nurse pots= enough of that talk now tomorrow we are going on a shopping trip and I want you all to be on your best behaviour so of to bed early tonight and get ready for tomorrow

Beth= nurse can I have a bath tonight

Smithy =so long as you leave the door open

Peter= is that all you think about is sex

Smithy=who asked you to butt in go and put your make up on and keep your mouth shut

Nurse pots=stop the bickering and yes Beth you can have a bath and not to much water on the floor and don't take all night

Beth= thanks nurse

Smithy=nurse can I have a stronger sleeping tablet tonight I can't sleep with Peter brown pacing across the floor all night

Nurse pots= you should read a book if you cannot sleep

Ed case= you can read some of my books

Smithy= I don't read dirty books

Nurse pots= come along now and get ready for your medication and smoke your last cigarette now

Peter=I am looking forward to my shopping trip tomorrow so I need my beauty sleep

Nurse pots= and that goes for all of you so come on and go to bed now 'Beth hurry up and dry yourself you have been in that bath all evening and we are all getting up early in the morning so get a move on

Beth= a girl has to look her best

Nurse pots= well you can go to bed now and you no the rules no smoking after ten

Beth= good night every one see you all tomorrow

Ed case= pleasant nightmares

Next day

And ward 11 is of on a shopping trip

Nurse pots=I want you all to go of on your own and meet me back in two hours at green lane cafe and don't be late

Peter= can I go round with you Beth because I need a blusher and some eye liner from boots

Smithy= just look at that women over there I think she as put on her make on with a trawl she must be about eighty

Peter= you want to take a look at your self smithy no body's perfect

Smithy= Speak for your self

Nurse pots= go on now and do your shopping and behave your selves

After the shopping trip when they all arrive back on ward 11

Nurse pots= what did you buy today Peter

Peter=I bought a blusher and some lipstick and it was buy one get one free

Smith= I bet he nicked the other ones

Beth= you should of come with us

Smithy= I would rather get arrested then go into a women's shop

Ed case= you nearly did Smithy for shoplifting

Smithy= shut up Ed and any way I can always plead insane

Peter= nurse I am feeling a bit hungry now and looking forward to my tea

Ed case= so long as its not meat balls or faggots

Nurse pots = no it is Sheppard's pie and rice pudding with jam so all of you get ready for your tea and I don't want to see no empty plates after tea we can have a game of bingo

Beth= legs eleven

Smithy= I am not playing

Nurse pots= why not

Smithy= in case my number is up

Peter= oh you are funny nurse can I call the numbers out

Ed case= number ten mp's hiding den

Beth= can we play connect four

Peter= that's for little children

Smithy= she is a little kid smoking behind the bike sheds she has never grown up nurse can I watch the football on telly

Peter= football is a load of balls

Smithy= at least it is a man's game

Ed case=I prefer women's football there much sexier

Beth= I hate foot ball is there any soaps on the box

Peter=yes East Enders

Smithy=that soap is to depressing for me and it scares me when they are all coming from the dead give me a good game of foot ball any day

Supper time

Nurse pots= come a long and get your coco and ginger biscuits
Peter=can I have extra medication tonight nurse I feel one of my turns is coming on
Nurse pots=you need to learn how to relax more
Ed case=he his missing his boyfriend
Peter=he his visiting me tomorrow
Smithy=well don't give him any beans because we don't want to be gassed again
Peter= oh you can be awful but we still love you
Smithy=careful Peter I am spoken for
Ed case=pleasant night mares everyone
Smithy=night night john boy
Beth=sweet dreams
Nurse pots= good night and god bless and may you all have a perfect day tomorrow

The end

Love your neighbours

Dolly parker was a busy old body always interfering in her neighbours business she never had a good word to say about any of her neighbours always complaining about Mr Jones singing at the top his voice when he came back home from the local pub who was a merry old soul and who wouldn't do any harm to anyone Dolly also complained about the local children playing football in the street the children nicknamed her nosey old parker the children would run away from her when she was walking down the street Dolly lived up to her nickname always complaining to the council on just about everything her neighbours did they wanted nothing to do with her but behind Dolly's lace curtains and her rein of terror was a very lonely old lady who longed for company but drove all her neighbours away instead she was a secret drinker drowning her sorrows night after night and no one never heard her or her cries for help. A few days later Mr Ali the local shopkeeper was getting concerned that he had not seen Dolly in his shop for a few days And asked Billy a neighbour to call round to Dolly's house to see if she was alright And when Billy got to Dolly's house it was all in darkness her curtains still drown in the middle of the afternoon which concerned Billy so he knocked on her door and when he got no answer he broke down the door and found Dolly unconscious and two empty whiskey bottles by her side Billy felt for a pulse And Dolly was barely alive so he called for a ambulance and Dolly was rushed to the local hospital where Billy stayed by Dolly's side through out the night Dolly had no family of her own so Billy acted as her guardian and when Dolly came round and saw Billy's face she just broke down and cried and saying how sorry she was Billy squeezed her hand and said to her you have nothing to be sorry about and the next few days Billy and Dolly became firm friends Dolly's neighbours had heard of Dolly's plight and wanted to offer there hand in friendship When Dolly came out of the hospital all her neighbours had cleaned her house and organised a welcome home party for her Dolly was getting to know her neighbours again and this time was full of praise for them and thanked them for all there kindness behind her mask had been a very sad old

lonely lady who almost drove her neighbours to despair the truth behind this story all Dolly wanted was her neighbours friendship and company so this story has a happy ending and if you know of a Dolly in your street just a few words of comfort and a helping hand which is all that is needed
So love your neighbours

Cheers